THE
ALPHABET PRAYER

By
LINDA SEGER
&
PETER LE VAR

Calligraphy by Matthew Wright

Clovercroft Publishing

The Alphabet Prayer

© 2016 by Linda Seger and Peter Le Var

Published by Clovercroft Publishing, Franklin, Tennessee

Published in association with Larry Carpenter of
Christian Book Services, LLC.
www.christianbookservices.com

Unless noted, all Scripture taken from THE HOLY BIBLE, NEW INTERNATIONAL VERSION®, NIV® Copyright © 1973, 1978, 1984, 2011 by Biblica, Inc.™ Used by permission. All rights reserved worldwide.

Cover Design by Nick Zelinger

Interior Design by Suzanne Lawing

Printed in the United States of America

978-1-942557-85-2

Endorsements

"*The Alphabet Prayer* is a beautifully contemplative book that draws me right into the arms of our loving God. Peter and Linda have clearly spent enough time in God's presence to offer us their prayers in this creative, effective, thoughtful devotional. It shows a depth of love, wisdom and peace in Peter and Linda that is beautiful! I love it and I hope everyone in my prayer network will embrace this book as a powerful way to both learn more about who God is and to experience how personally He loves each one of us."

> —**KAREN COVELL**, PRODUCER AND FOUNDING DIRECTOR OF THE HOLLYWOOD PRAYER NETWORK

"I commend Peter and Linda for the simple format of a Scripture quote, followed by a reflection leading into the artfully stated prayer to the One with many names. There is an invitation here for a lifetime of intimate loving dialog with the Divine – all done in the Lectio Divina format."

> —**SISTER THERESE O'GRADY**, OSB, BENET HILL MONASTERY

As a former Catholic and then Southern Protestant, currently a sometimes Episcopalian, professional Mythologist, and practicing Agnostic, I find Peter and Linda's *Alphabet Prayer* book a delightful, perceptive, and engaging collection of perspectives on our relationship with spiritual truths. Ranging from the deeply personal to the politely pleading to the freely praising, there is something here for the benefit of people of any spiritual awareness, regardless of your religious affiliation or the lack thereof. As a Comparative Mythologist, I find their approach, though drawn from the writings of the Bible, to be Universal. The invitation to Reflection sections could be used in any setting by individuals or organizations. It's rich wisdom, presented against the background of one of the world's major religions but not bound to it at all offers a powerful dose of daily inspiration. The authors stand like those valiant and generous archetypes found in most mythologies – those who have seen a Light and hold the door open and point the way for the rest of us to see it, too.

—**PAMELA JAYE SMITH**, AUTHOR, INTER-
NATIONAL SPEAKER AND CONSULTANT,
AWARD-WINNING PRODUCER-DIRECTOR.

"Combining visual and spiritual beauty, 'The Alphabet Prayer Book' will have broad appeal as both esthetic treat and inspirational source."

—**DR. JEAN VAIL**, AUTHOR, *EXPLORING GOD'S
LOVE IN PRAYER AND PULPIT*

"Matt Wright is one of the most talented calligraphy students in my many years of teaching. There are wonderful subtleties to his work which treat each prayer uniquely without detracting from the message."

—**TIMOTHY R. BOTTS**, CALLIGRAPHIC ARTIST AND AUTHOR

"How refreshing it is to see a book using calligraphy to express the meaning of its content of quotations. Most publishers don't appreciate how the handwritten word can add depth to visual dimension and meaning compared with type. Calligraphy is particularly appropriate for a book of prayers because medieval manuscripts are mostly associated with biblical texts. Here Matt Wright shows mastery of many modernized historical styles of script, spanning 2,000 years of the development of Western writing. The feeling of the words for each letter and short text of the alphabet is reflected in his choice of style, so there are twenty-six styles or variations of style, while adhering to the unifying format of a large initial letter above the short text below it, on each right hand page. Colors vary according to the atmosphere author and scribe have created. To leaf through this book is to see something different in our present age and is a really enjoyable surprise, showing that calligraphy can stand alone and do its creative job without the need of supportive illustrations."

—**SHEILA WATERS**, CALLIGRAPHER AND AUTHOR OF *FOUNDATIONS OF CALLIGRAPHY*

"What a joy to peruse this lovely devotional book written by a couple deeply committed to the life of the Spirit Its message of God's love and grace inspires and comforts, enhanced by beautiful calligraphy, meaningful bible passages, and wise, heart-opening questions and advices. I recommend this book to anyone seeking a way to reconnect with Spirit, especially during difficult times."

—**ANTHONY MANOUSOS**, PEACE ACTIVIST, AUTHOR OF *TRANSFORMATIVE FRIENDS*, AND SPIRITUAL DIRECTOR

Dedication

Dedicated to the Colorado Springs Friends Meeting,
our spiritual community that has loved and nurtured us.

Acknowledgements

Thank you to Matt Wright for his elegant artistry and his knowledge of historical and contemporary calligraphy.

Thank you to our readers who have given us feedback throughout the years: Timothy Botts, Brooks Graebner, Cathleen Loeser, Pamela Jaye Smith, and Sue Terry.

Thank you to our assistant, Katie Davis Gardner, for her constructive response, her reliability, and all her good work.

Introduction

In May, 2001, I was ready to start a vacation of horseback riding and fun at one of our favorite guest ranches. On the first day of our vacation, while bending over to look at the label of a very comfortable mattress, I stood up and suddenly felt a "shlup" in my lower back. I had just had a serious accident and soon discovered I had herniated two discs in my back.

In the ensuing weeks, the pain was, at times, excruciating. I was disappointed to have missed my much-needed vacation. I was frustrated about my inability to work. And I regretted the many problems my disability caused my wife. Yet, all I could do was be still, see the doctor daily, and bear it. As I lay healing, several comments were made to me: "Poor Peter!" "How can you stand doing nothing?" "In your shoes, I'd go completely nuts!"

Of course, to incur injury is always difficult. Constraint became a normal part of my everyday life. The pain of the injury was crippling and overwhelming. I had little choice but to do nothing. Resistance to the injury would only have exacerbated the condition.

Quieting down seemed more nurturing than acting up. My years spent as a Quaker learning to listen and ponder in silent worship came to aid me. Three decades of undisciplined transcendental meditation now served to help me center and focus on releasing physical dis-ease quite easily. I prayed to the God I knew and know. At one point I distinctly felt the remarkable hand of God.

I had read the Bible before, but now I turned to Psalms and the Gospels with which I felt healing reverberations. I prayed. I visualized healing. Many times I felt these tools more significant to the healing process than much of the medical treatment.

I discovered being disabled could contribute to spiritual development. My disability allowed those close to me to express their goodness in helping me with my needs.

While I was healing, I began a ritual of prayer. First I'd recite The Lord's Prayer and the Prayer of Jabez. Then, I delivered my own prayers, expressing my needs and wants. And then I found myself creating a different kind of prayer - *The Alphabet Prayer.*

In the past, I used to say a prayer whenever I traveled in an airplane: Mother/Father God, please embrace this airplane, the pilot, copilot and navigator, embrace each and every attendant and each and every passenger. In order to remember all my requests, I alphabetized them: God, Embrace them in your Care and Comfort, in your Direction, in your Goodness and Guidance, in your Light and Love.

During my disability, I began creating an Alphabet Prayer for healing. I eventually mentioned my Alphabet Prayer to my wife. Linda replied, "Honey, I think you have a book!" Linda, who is a trained theologian and an author, suggested we could add to it further by drawing on the many names of God from Christianity, Judaism, and Islam. In short, Linda opened up the alphabet prayer to some wonderful other possibilities.

Thus, dear reader and dear pray-er, I offer to you my alphabet prayer. I offer it to you in your times of trial and tribulation and in your times of challenge and joy. I offer it into the experience of your life that you may be enriched by it, as my life has been. I hope these prayers are as comforting and expanding to you as they've been to me. Perhaps, like me, you'll memorize them and meditate on them. I hope they lead you to add your own words and prayers to mine.

Peter Hazen Le Var

The Scripture

*Your hands made me and formed me;
give me understanding to learn your commands.*

PSALM 119:73

Invitation To Reflection

Authority can sometimes feel oppressive, as if someone is controlling us and manipulating us and suppressing our talents and desires. How can God be my authority, while still freeing me to be my own individual person? How can my awareness of God's authority lead me to a stronger relationship with God? Since God is Infinite Goodness and Wisdom and Possibilities, then only by allowing God to inhabit our lives, do we truly become free, and do we truly become who we were created to become.

Almighty God,
Awaken me to an awareness of
Your absolute authority
and my absolute
accountability to You.

The Scripture

You welcome him with rich blessings
and placed a crown of pure gold on his head...
Surely you have granted him eternal blessings,
and made him glad with the joy of your presence.

PSALM 21: 3, 6

Invitation To Reflection

How difficult is it for you to ask God for blessings? Does it seem selfish to ask for God to bring you an abundant, bountiful life? When you are truly blessed, do you notice?

The Prayer of Jabez asks that God bring him many blessings. A Quaker theologian, Howard Brinton tells us to pray about whatever we want. If the prayer is selfish, God will change the prayer while we are praying. Imagine praying for, and being showered with, God's bounty, beauty and blessings. Imagine the Beneficent God desiring to give you all good gifts.

Beneficent One

Bring me bounty,
beauty and blessings.

The Scripture

*Be at rest once more, O my soul,
for the Lord has been good to you.*

PSALM 116:7

Invitation To Reflection

As you pray this prayer, notice your breathing. Is it slowing down? Do you feel a gentle comfort washing over you? Can you sense the comfort that comes from The Compassionate God that knows your condition and calms you and comforts you, before helping you resolve any issues that threaten to overwhelm you?

Before resolving any crisis, God needs to be in our quiet center. As you pray this prayer several times, see if you can feel God's Comforting Presence.

Compassionate One

calm me

and

comfort me

The Scripture

My soul finds rest in God alone;
my salvation comes from him.
He alone is my rock, and my salvation.
He is my fortress, I will never be shaken.

PSALM 62:1-2

Invitation To Reflection

We often think of God as guiding us toward a goal, or leading us to do God's will. Imagine God deepening you first, creating within you the values and courage and love you will need to be directed toward a goal. Imagine God defending and protecting those qualities, preparing you, so you can do God's work in the world.

DIVINE DELIVERER

DEEPEN ME

DIRECT ME

DEFEND ME

The Scripture

Lord, you have been our dwelling place,
throughout all generations.

PSALM 90:1

Invitation To Reflection

Rarely do most of us think of a sensual relationship with God. Yet *The Song of Solomon* is filled with sensual images that can be interpreted metaphorically as God's love of us and God's yearning for a relationship with us. The Church fills the air with incense and the rich hues of stained glass windows and the knobby or soft textures of religious tapestries. Imagine being filled and surrounded by the essence of God. For you, is it a smell? A feeling? An image? Can you imagine being enfolded by this essence forever?

Exalted One,

Embrace me and enrich me

with your essence from

everlasting to everlasting.

The Scripture

Hear, O Lord, and answer me,
for I am poor and needy …
You are forgiving and good, O Lord,
abounding in love to all who call to you….
Teach me your way, O Lord,
and I will walk in your truth;
give me an undivided heart,
that I may fear your name.…
For great is your love toward me;
you have delivered me from the depths of the grave.…
But you, O Lord,
are a compassionate and gracious God,
slow to anger, abounding in love and faithfulness

PSALM 86: 1, 5, 11, 13, 15

Invitation To Reflection

It can be difficult to imagine God's complete forgiveness of our flaws, mistakes, sins, wrong-doings, and pigheadedness. Imagine being so completely forgiven, that you would then turn around and ask the person you've wronged to then grant you a favor. Imagine having the Faith to believe that's exactly what God wants to do. What in your life needs to be forgiven? What faith and favor do you need that will renew you and make you whole again?

forgiving father,
feed me
with
faith and favor.

The Scripture

Give thanks to the Lord, for he is good;
his love endures forever.

PSALM 118:29

Invitation To Reflection

What do we need in order to be generous people? We need to have something to give and the willingness to give it. If we feel scarcity in our lives, or competition with others, or a lack of love for others, we are unable to make the leap to giving. We may feel our giving can deplete us rather than fulfill us. Yet if a gracious God is constantly fulfilling us, and asking us to be an instrument and vessel of God's glorious generosity, we can freely give. How difficult is it for you to trust in God's generosity? How much of God's grace are you able to allow to move through you so you can be generous with others?

Gracious and glorious God,

grant me the gift of generosity

and gratitude.

The Scripture

*He heals the brokenhearted
and binds up their wounds.*

PSALM 147:3

Invitation To Reflection

Have you ever felt you were falling to pieces? The poet, W.B. Yeats uses the line, "The Center cannot hold." When we are sick, nothing seems to work right. And we can be unhealthy on so many levels – physical, mental, professional, personal, spiritual. Being well means being integrated, having one's life in one piece, working toward a clear goal and in a right relationship with God and with those around us. What in your life is out of sorts? What would it look like and feel like to be whole again? Can you imagine yourself well and functioning as a happy and healthy person? Can you pray this prayer, while thinking of those pieces you want God to heal and make whole?

holy one,
and
wholly one,

heal me
and make me
whole.

The Scripture

Great is the Lord, and most worthy of praise;
his greatness no one can fathom.

PSALM 145:3

Invitation To Reflection

Sometimes we think of being filled with the Holy Spirit. Have you ever thought of being immersed in God? Imagine the Presence of God around you, within you, above you, behind you, before you, embracing you. To Inspire is to "breathe in". Imagine breathing in God – a God who is so immediate and inexhaustible He cannot be exhaled. Imagine God, the Inexhaustible, The Always Present.

Immanent and
immediate God,
immerse me
in your inexhaustible
inspiration.

The Scripture

Because of the oppression of the weak
and the groaning of the needy,
I will now arise, says the Lord. I will protect them
from those who malign them.

PSALM 12:5

Invitation To Reflection

The Gospel, without the social Gospel, is not the complete Good News. God's work of making the World, and us, in right relationship to ourselves, to each other, and to God, is a journey of justice. How do you feel about the evils and problems and flaws in the world? Overwhelmed? Helpless? Uncaring? Are they outside your vision – or just a blur of chaos? What are the special problems you care about, and the ones you don't? What happens to your perception of the problems, and your action to help solve these problems, when you join the Just Judge to be part of the solution?

JUST JUDGE

JOIN ME
TO YOUR JOURNEY
FOR JUSTICE

You guide me with your counsel,
and afterward you will take me into glory.

PSALM 73:24

Invitation To Reflection

In Genesis, Adam and Eve walk with God in the cool of the evening. He is their kindred spirit, who cares for them, protects them, and embraces them as a Good Creation. Imagine God as a companion who embraces you with care and loving-kindness. Does a God who is this close and intimate frighten you, challenge you, or enthrall you?

KIND AND KINDRED SPIRIT,

KEEP ME IN THY CARE.

The Scripture

You, O Lord, keep my lamp burning;
my God turns my darkness into light.

PSALM 18:28

Invitation To Reflection

Think about how you respond to Light. Does it refresh you? Perk you up? Give you energy? Have you ever played with light, watching it make patterns on the walls, the floor, or on the face of another? God has been compared to a Light, a light that pierces the darkness, and also a light that we wait for, as if waiting for the dawn that will give us new energy and new beginnings.

Is there any part of your life that yearns for God's light to heal you? To energize you? To lead you? To dance and move with you?

Lord of love

enliven me with your

life-giving light

The Scripture

How many are your works, O Lord!
In wisdom you made them all;
The earth is full of your creatures...
When you send your Spirit, they are created,
and you renew the face of the earth.

PSALM 104:24, 30

Invitation To Reflection

We are created, molded, and shaped by God. Yet, instead of thinking of ourselves as part of God's glorious creation, sometimes we consider ourselves as nothing, a worm, a miniscule and unworthy object. But God's doesn't make junk.

When you think of yourself as purposefully shaped by God, does this give you the inspiration to manifest God's Goodness and Love?

Most magnificent master,

make me mindful that
you are my maker
that I may magnify
and manifest you.

The Scripture

The Lord is my Shepherd, I shall not want.
He makes me lie down in green pastures.
He leads me beside quiet waters,
He restores my soul…
Surely goodness and love will follow
me all the days of my life.

PSALM 23: 1-3, 6

Invitation To Reflection

Have you experienced the nurturing of God? Has it come as comfort? Encouragement? Healing? A sense of a loving presence? A quieting? A strengthening? When have you been able to nurture others as God has nurtured you? Did you feel a connection between God's work in your life and how you allowed God to work through you?

NUMINOUS NURTURER

NUDGE ME
AND ENABLE ME
TO NURTURE OTHERS
AS YOU HAVE
NOURISHED ME

The Scripture

Praise God in his sanctuary;
Praise him in his mighty heavens.
Praise him for his acts of power;
Praise him for his surpassing greatness.

PSALM 150: 1-2

Invitation To Reflection

Does the power of God make you bow in love, or fear? Are you ever afraid of the ever-watchful eyes of God? Are you thankful for God's constant presence? Do you truly believe in God's power, and live your life accordingly? Or do you sometimes doubt whether God is near, or so powerful in a world that sometimes seems to be without the presence of Good? Imagine offering homage to the All-Powerful God. Does it make you feel empowered?

Omnipotent, omniscient, and omnipresent God, originator of all,

I offer you homage and obedience.

The Scripture

Turn from evil and do good;
seek peace and pursue it.

PSALM 34:14

Invitation To Reflection

We cry out for peace, but there is no peace. Why is it so difficult to choose the path of peace, for ourselves and for our world? What within you is violent? Warring? Hostile? Filled with animosity? What within our world are the barriers to peace? Is it possible for you to persevere on the path to peace, even when others do not?

Patient and
powerful presence,

empower me

to persevere on your path

toward peace.

The Scripture

Show me your ways, O Lord, teach me your paths;
guide me in your truth and teach me,
for you are God my Savior,
and my hope is in you all day long.

PSALM 25:4-5

Invitation To Reflection

What do you do to achieve a good life, a life of quality? Do you engage in a flurry of activity, trying to make everything right and good for you and others? To what extent is quietness part of your quest for quality? As you pray this prayer, hold two thoughts in your mind: the good life you desire, and the centered quietness of rest before your pursuit of excellence. Like the runner who is still and takes deep breaths before sprinting toward a goal, we need to recognize the balance between stillness and action, in the quest we share with God.

QUINTESSENTIAL GOD,

QUIET ME, QUICKEN ME, IN YOUR QUEST FOR QUALITY.

The Scripture

My soul finds rest in God alone;
my salvation comes from him.
He alone is my rock and my salvation;
he is my fortress, I will never be shaken.
PSALM 62:1-2

Invitation To Reflection

Where do you run to when you feel in trouble? When scared? Pursued? Betrayed? Accused? When we run to God, not only are we protected, but God can empower us and change what we need changed in order to restore us to a right relationship with ourselves and with those we perceive as our enemies. Imagine having the courage to go back into the fray, because God has been your refuge, and has empowered you and restored you to make it possible for you to go on.

Redeemer,
my rock, and my refuge,
restore me
to righteousness.

The Scripture

Your right hand sustains me; you stoop down to make me great. You broaden the path beneath me, so that my ankles do not turn.
PSALM 18: 35-36

Invitation To Reflection

We can only respond with what we have within us. If we haven't developed our spiritual life, and developed our ability to manifest goodness, mercy, compassion, and love in this world, we have little to give. What is the substance and the sustenance you need from God to fill you up to overflowing, so you can serve God?

SAVIOR

**SUSTAIN ME
WITH YOUR SUBSTANCE
AND SUSTENANCE
SO I CAN BETTER
SERVE THEE**

The Scripture

Surely you desire truth in the inner parts;
You teach me wisdom in the inmost place.
PSALM 51:6

Invitation To Reflection

Are there times in your life when you don't want to know God's truth, but would rather do it your own way? What part of God's truth is difficult for you? That we should love one another, even our enemies? That God is our creator and that we manifest God's goodness? That we are asked to live together in unity and peace with each other? Imagine being turned and tuned to live all parts of your life in truth.

Transcendent
and
transforming God,

turn us and tune us
to your truth.

The Scripture

*How good and pleasant it is when brothers
(all people) live together in unity!*
PSALM 133:1

Invitation To Reflection

We live in a divided world where our adversaries are often anyone who is different from us. Are there people in this world who you feel you don't understand? You dislike? You see as your enemies? Are they Christians? Jews? Muslims? Buddhists? Middle Easterners? Southerners? Yankees? Africans? The Chinese? The Koreans? Think about all those you have trouble imagining as your brothers and sisters. Imagine welcoming them into unity with you.

Universal
and
Ubiquitous
God

Unite us
in Understanding
and
Uprightness

The Scripture

The Lord watches over you –
the Lord is your shade at your right hand;…
The Lord will keep you from all harm –
he will watch over your life;
the Lord will watch over your coming and going,
both now and forevermore.
PSALM 121: 5, 7, 8

Invitation To Reflection

Do you ever feel victimized by evil? Have you ever felt in the clutches of evil? Or uneasy and overcome by something you can't name, but that just feels wrong? How much do you feel you have to fight to overcome evil? How does prayer and meditating on God's presence diminish the power of evil in your life so you are not a victim of the dark?

Valiant and victorious God,

help me be
vigilant and prevail,
that I may not be
a victim of evil.

The Scripture

I will extol the Lord with all my heart in the
council of the upright and in the assembly...
Great are the works of the Lord;...
The fear of the Lord is the beginning of wisdom;
all who follow his precepts have good understanding.
To him belongs eternal praise.
PSALM 111:1, 2, 10

Invitation To Reflection

The Greek word for wisdom is Sophia, who is described by King Solomon as discerning and as a delight. Some call her the feminine face of God. Wisdom desires to work with us. She waits for us, and watches over us, like a mother warming her brood of chicks. Imagine Wisdom guiding you, as she guided Solomon, to do God's will.

Wise one,

watch over me,

and grant me wisdom

that I may be a witness

and willing partner

to your will.

The Scripture

...I have stilled and quieted my soul;
like a weaned child with its mother,
like a weaned child is my soul within me.
PSALM 131:2

Invitation To Reflection

What are your metaphors for God? Although God is usually referred to as "He" in the Bible, in Judaism one of the many names for God is Rakhamon, which means both The Compassionate One and the Womb. In both Hebrew and Greek, the word for the Holy Spirit (Shekinah) and the word for the Wisdom of God (Sophia) are female words. In the Bible, God is sometimes compared to a mother hen who cares for her chicks, or compared with a woman seeking her lost coin as God seeks us. God is also referred to with gender-neutral words, such as Light, Rock, Dove of Peace, and The Divine Mystery. How does it expand how you see God by adding to your metaphors of God? Can you imagine yielding to the comfort of the nurturing Mother, sharing yourself with the Beloved Friend, and being yoked to the loving Father?

Gender-ful God,

who made us in your image,
male and female,
you who are everything to us –
father, mother, brother,
sister, beloved, friend.

God beyond gender
– the mystery,

I yearn for you,
teach me to yield to you
and be yoked to you.

The Scripture

…Zeal for your house consumes me, …
PSALM 69:9

Invitation To Reflection

Some people speak of being "on fire for the Lord". Others of being partners with a Dancing God. Others of the Flame of the Holy Spirit burning within them. Do you see a difference between zest for life and a zest for God? Are you zealous to manifest some particular attributes of God in this world - God's love? God's Justice? God's Forgiveness? God's Acceptance? God's healing power? God's Peace? God's Joy? What would it mean for you to have a life of zest and zeal?

Zealous God,

grant me

zest and zeal.

About the Authors:

Peter and Linda met in Quaker Meeting and were married in Santa Monica Friends Meeting in April, 1987. Both Peter and Linda are Christians.

Dr. Linda Seger is the granddaughter of a Lutheran minister with a family tree that includes ministers, missionaries and theologians for a number of generations. She began studying theology in the 1960's and attended seminary from 1971 to 1976. In 1973, she received an M.A. in Religion and the Arts. In 1976, she received a ThD in Drama and Theology and in 2000, she received an M.A. in Feminist Theology. She has brought her broad theological background to this prayer book, including her work in systematic theology, liberation theology, feminist theology, process theology and creation theology. Linda is the author of nine books in the field of screenwriting and film, and six spiritual books including: *The Better Way to Win: Connecting, not Competing, for Success,* (2011), *Jesus Rode a Donkey: Why Millions of Christians are Democrats,* (2006), *Spiritual Steps on the Road to Success: Gaining the Goal Without Losing Your Soul,* (2009), *What Our Mamas Taught Us,* (2015), and *Reflections with God While Waiting to be Healed* (2017).

Peter Hazen Le Var grew up Presbyterian, and began attending Quaker Meeting in 1983. He has been a licensed massage therapist since 1980, and has taught massage therapy and shiatsu. In 2000, he received his M.A.

in Acupuncture and Chinese Herbology. His spirituality has deepened through the healing he's received as a result of several work-related health problems. He created *The Alphabet Prayer* as a way to center, meditate, and pray when recovering from a herniated disk throughout much of 2001.

About the Calligrapher:

Matt Wright graduated from Greenville College in 2003 with a degree in Fine Arts and continues to be mentored by his former professor Steven Heilmer. His work consists of a wide range of media including painting, drawing, and ceramics. In 2008, he decided to try his hand at calligraphy, and he immediately fell in love with letterforms. He was taught and is mentored by Timothy Botts. Matt's interest initially was in learning historical scripts but over the last several years, he has been exploring modern lettering and experimental letterforms.

Matt is dyslexic so being drawn toward letterforms was a peculiar pursuit, since words and reading had always been his Achilles' heel. Calligraphy in the West hasn't typically been associated with Fine Art, but Matt's main concern is using calligraphy as a lens for conceptual exploration. He has also been learning stone letter carving.

Matt has been married to Nikki since 2002, and they have two sons, Mason and Landon.

Calligraphy Scripts

A – Gothicized Italic

B – Rhythmic Italic

C – Half Uncial

D – Rustic

E – Pointed Pen Script

F – Carolingian

G – Italic Variation

H – Uncial

I – Pen Manipulated Italic

J – Roman brush lettered

K – Rhythmic Italic Capitals

L – Legende

M – Flourished Italic with bracketed serifs

N – Roman Variation

O – Blackletter

P – Pressurized Foundational

Q – Modern Roman brush lettered

R – Fraktur

S – Neuland

T – Classical Italic

U – Uncial and Roman Hybrid

V – Foundational

W – Copperplate

X/Y – Bookhand with serifs and sans serif

Z - Fraktur